Water Beasties Across the Seas

Ever look out at the water and wonder what's beneath?

Mermaids or kraken?

People didn't believe giant squid existed, until they discovered that they were real…

Cities under the seas

Lost civilizations galore—at least stories about them. How much truth is behind those tales?

**Take a journey
around the world with us and explore water beasts
wherever we go**

Workshops by Eilis Flynn and Jacquie Rogers

The Silk Road Myths and Legends Workshop Series
Angels
Demons
Dragons
Faeries
Ghosts
Vampires
Water Beasties
Werewolves and Other Shapeshifters
Zombies

The Five Stages of Editing Grief
Geeks and Gamers' Guide to Worldbuilding

Books by Eilis Flynn and Jacquie Rogers

Ghosts Along the Silk Road and Beyond
Dragons Along the Silk Road and Beyond
Vampires and Zombies Along the Silk Road
Water Beasties Across the Seven Seas
Werewolves and Other Shapeshifters Along the Silk Road
(forthcoming)

WATER BEASTIES ACROSS THE SEVEN SEAS

*Based on the series of workshops presented by
Eilis Flynn and Jacquie Rogers*

Eilis Flynn
and
Jacquie Rogers

Water Beasties Beyond the Seven Seas

Cover design: Melissa Russell
Original cover design by Jacquie Rogers
ISBN-13: 9798419438491

For Mike and Mark.
Thank you.

Thanks to Joelle Izack and Sonya Rhen, who were kind enough to give us thoughtful and useful feedback to make this book better.

Chapters

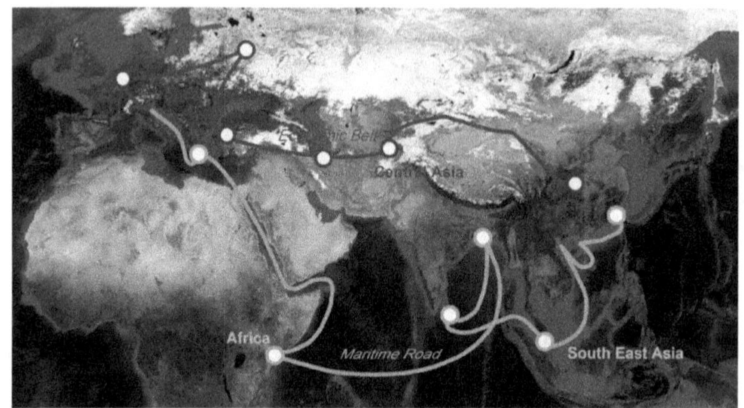

A map for the Silk Road journey.

Introduction
*Water, Water Everywhere and
Mysterious Beasts in It All*

Water, water everywhere, and mysterious beasts in all of it!
The planet is mostly water, and even though we have
landed on the moon and some parts beyond, we still are
painfully aware that we don't know everything that's in the
seas right here on Earth. Each time we think there's nothing
more to be revealed in its depths, something new and
surprising comes out of it, in the form of something that
was assumed to be extinct tens of thousands of years ago,
or with its only known relatives 500 million years old. Every
time we hear about the Loch Ness monster being fictional,
we hear about a real prehistoric fish discovered still around.
For every Nessie, we have something like a coelacanth,
thought to have become extinct in the Cretaceous period,
but found alive and well and thriving today!

Our planet's been explored pretty thoroughly since
mankind's been around, from the top of Mt. Everest all the
way down to…okay, not so much the seven seas. Every
time we turn around, we read about some form of sea life
thought to have been extinct for tens of thousands of years
being caught by a fisherman right here in the present day.

The oceans are truly the final undiscovered country of
planet Earth, and they've been feared and respected in equal
parts as long as mankind has been around, spinning tales

about what could possibly dwell down below. From the sinister kappa that await in the rivers to attack the unsuspecting human in Japan to the water ghosts of the Nordic countries, join us as we take a trip around the world in a glass-bottomed boat and see what awaits us under the sea. Water, water everywhere, but it's always been mysterious. And as always, what people don't understand, they make up stories.

Some of you may be familiar with workshops that we have presented. If you're not, basically, it's like this: We came up with this series of workshops when we realized there were variations of the same myths all around the world, and it would be a great way to inspire writers to tell their stories. Eilis was an anthropology major, so she knew that cultures that were in the same region or came from the same roots would usually have similar legends and myths, and she'd already spent some time analyzing them, noting how they changed as the cultures did. She comes from Japanese stock and writes Asian-based fantasies, while Jacquie has done a good deal of research on European mythologies for her series of fantasy romances. We decided to combine all that and look at the myths along the Silk Road and around the world, this time looking at water creatures. This book is designed to be a prompt. Use it as an inspiration for all the stories you want to tell.

And before we get started, let us tell you about the Silk Road. Traditionally, the Silk Road was a series of important trading routes going over land and sea that existed long before the Christian era began. A *lot* of trade occurred along those routes, bringing silks and spices and more from the East to the West, and vice versa.

The Silk Road connected a region of China with Asia Minor and the Mediterranean, a route that was more than 5,000 miles long—a fair distance these days, but unimaginable back then, fraught with danger and a round-trip journey that took a very, very long time. The Silk Road had northern routes and southern routes, and the goods were transported from places as far away as the Philippines and Thailand and Brunei, all the way to Italy and Portugal and even Scandinavia.

Not only were silks and spices moved along these routes, so was culture, language, and even technology, and that meant Asian concepts and items were introduced to Europe, and vice versa. We'll see how those ideas began and changed as we travel from region to region, changing bit by bit until those concepts end up drastically different when compared side by side.

We're going to start in the most unlikely of beginnings: Hollywood!

~Eilis Flynn
Jacquie Rogers

Movie poster for the classic monster movie.

Chapter 1
Hooray for Watery Hollywood!

We'll start out in Hollywood and take a look at some of the movies that have fascinated us over the years that are about the Creatures of the Deep. IMDb messed up their search to make it "easier" (for whom?!) so it's difficult to find the older ones, and hey, we weren't around in 1895 when Georges Méliès was the hottest thing going in film, so unlike the other classes we teach, this chapter won't have much filmmaking history in it.

We didn't find all that many sea creature films (a few hundred compared to three thousand-plus dragon movies) and it occurred to us that watery critters mean two things: a bigger budget is required, and you have to dunk your stars, which messes up their makeup and hairdos. Also, the technology for underwater filming was far more complicated, as opposed to now (computers have been a huge boon for TV and movies).

That said, let's go to the movies! There are many movies and TV shows involving the water and its secret beasties, and here's just a handful:

20,000 Leagues Under the Sea (1916, 1954, 1985, and again in 1997, and more to come)
This is probably the most famous sea creature film, adapted from a classic novel by Jules Verne. The villain in

this movie starts out to be a vicious narwhal, which isn't a fictitious creature, then the protagonists, played by Kirk Douglas, Paul Lucas, and Peter Lorre in the 1954 version, discover the villain is actually a submarine—the *Nautilus* with Captain Nemo at the helm. But even the submarine is attacked by a giant squid. Keep in mind that in 1954, giant squid were still thought to be fictitious.

Mr. Peabody and the Mermaid (1948)
Based on the novel *Peabody's Mermaid*, this fantasy starred William Powell and Ann Blyth, and sequences were shot at the Weeki Wachee Springs in Florida (see Chapter 8 for more about the mermaids of Weeki Wachee!).

Creature from the Black Lagoon (1954)
A scary water beastie really is in this picture starring Richard Carlson, Julie Adams, and Richard Denning. From IMDb: "A scientific expedition searching for fossils along the Amazon River discovers a prehistoric Gill-Man in the legendary Black Lagoon." There's more than a touch of King Kong in this, because the water beastie falls in love with the fiancée of one of the explorers and kidnaps her. Sounds like it would fit right in with today's paranormal romance readers. (This movie apparently inspired in part an Academy Award–winning movie later on, *The Shape of Water*, in 2017!)

Voyage to the Bottom of the Sea (1961)
The 1961 movie was so popular that they made a TV series spinoff. We'll talk about the movie because as you can guess, the TV series was simply a quest to find the Water Beastie of the Week (but we have fond memories of it). The movie starred Walter Pidgeon, Joan Fontaine, and Barbara Eden, and the TV version starred Richard Basehart and David Hedison. No water creatures show up in the

synopsis but the gist is that scary critters fill in the blanks of suspense when the political intrigue flags. That's easy to do because the ocean holds us mystified, and maybe a little terrified to this day.

Splash! (1984)
This romantic comedy charmer, about a mermaid who finds herself in New York City, was a hit for Tom Hanks and Daryl Hannah. No scary beasties here, but if you have a soft touch for New York City, Tom Hanks, romantic comedies, or fantasies, it's going to be right up your alley. We enjoyed it a lot.

The Little Mermaid (1985)
Jacquie confesses that she's never read the story by Hans Christian Andersen and we all know that Disney takes massive liberties with fairytales. Andersen's original tale is much darker with a distinctly Judeo-Christian bent, where Ariel yearns for eternal life just as much as she does for love. In the story, the tone is much darker, and [spoiler] after Ariel trades her voice for her legs, endures pain, and doesn't get her man, she does get eternal life. Sort of. That's her happily ever after (HEA). In the movie, Disney tells a much more romantic tale and we all know she and the handsome prince live happily all the rest of their days. Of course, you need to listen to the melody "Kiss de Girl."

Secret of Roan Inish (1994)
Ten-year-old Fiona is sent to live with her grandparents in a small fishing village in Donegal, Ireland. She soon learns the local legend that an ancestor of hers married a selkie—a seal who can turn into a human. Years earlier, her baby brother washed out to sea in a cradle shaped like a boat; someone in the family believes the boy is being raised by seals. Then Fiona catches sight of a naked little boy on

the abandoned isle of Roan Inish and takes an active role in uncovering its secret. A monster? Nah, but it's a nice story.

Waterworld (1995)

The water beastie in this story is actually the hero played by Kevin Costner. His character, the Mariner, is a post-apocalyptic mutant. In this movie, Earth is mostly covered with water because both polar caps have melted. And of course there's thievery, shenanigans, and romance. Don't tell anyone, but we liked this movie.

Sphere (1998)

Michael Crichton's *Sphere* keeps us on edge when a spaceship is discovered at the bottom of the ocean, embedded in a 300-year-old layer of coral. Dustin Hoffman, Sharon Stone, and Samuel L. Jackson star in the film. There are a bunch of critters in this one, starting with a man-eating jellyfish, then a giant squid, sea snakes, and back to the squid. Again, the sea creatures may or may not be part of the science fiction mystery at various times, but because of our inherent fear factor, they up the ante considerably.

Kraken: Tentacles of the Deep (2006)

Here we have a genuine fur-lined sea monster movie, a B movie, for sure, but hey, you can't get better than the kraken. Charlie O'Connell, Victoria Pratt, and Kristi Angus star in this little-known production. IMDb's description: "Thirty years ago, Ray Reiter witnessed the brutal death of his parents at sea by a strange, octopus-like creature. Now determined to exact revenge, he joins archaeologist Nicole on a perilous high-seas expedition to find the legendary Greek Opal—said to be guarded by the very beast that murdered his family. As they come face to face with the killer kraken, they must also battle a ruthless crime lord, who will stop at nothing to seize the coveted treasure for himself." Bring popcorn.

The Water Horse (2007)
A lonely boy discovers a mysterious egg that hatches a water beastie of Scottish legend. Charming!

Ondine (2009)
Based on the classic story, this movie starring Colin Farrell is about an Irish fisherman who discovers a woman in his fishing net whom his precocious daughter believes to be a selkie. If only! (And yes, we did notice that both stories mentioned here involving selkies are Irish-based. Make of that as you will, but stories about selkies are generally Celtic and Norse in origin.)

Pirates of the Caribbean: On Stranger Tides (2011)
This installment of the adventures of, well, the pirates of the Caribbean, introduces new and old twists on the legends of the mermaids, as well as mysterious women, a quest for the fountain of youth, and fighting old foes and new.

Percy Jackson: Sea of Monsters (2013)
Taken from the novel by Rick Riordan, this is the story of a son of Poseidon, Percy Jackson, who has to procure the Golden Fleece from the Sea of Monsters. The star of the Sea of Monsters is, of course, Charybdis, who lives under a rock and can create very scary whirlpools (more about Charybdis later).

Sharknado ad infinitum (2013)
With this scarily terrible and scarily popular not to mention scarily funny TV movie and then its (five!) sequels, the premise is a massive waterspout swoops up sharks from

the sea and drops them onto innocent bystanders on land and chaos ensues. This series made us wonder if the humor was intentional or deliberate. But who are we to criticize? They made money, enough for *five!* sequels! They're memorable!

Song of the Sea (2014)

Directed by Tomm Moore, in this sweet animated movie, a young Irish girl who can turn into a seal and her brother go on a mission to free the faeries and save the spirit world!

The Shape of Water (2017)

This highly acclaimed film is reckoned to be a romantic fantasy, about a mute woman who falls in love with a humanoid amphibian creature who is being kept in a government facility. The American Film Institute called it one of the best films of the year, and it won Academy Awards for best picture, best director, best production design, and best original score. The director, Guillermo del Toro, apparently has said that he had fond memories of having seen *The Creature from the Black Lagoon*, and wanted to see a happy ending for that ill-fated romance. (This is how many authors end up writing, after all—to right the wrongs of sad endings!)

The Meg (2018)

This science-fiction movie came out in 2018, in which a group of scientists is threatened by a 75-foot-long megalodon shark on the floor of the Pacific Ocean. Predictably, it was a financial success but got mixed reviews—but a sequel is in development, so it's got that going for it.

Aquaman (2018)

We have an entire chapter devoted to Aquaman and his comics cohort later on. Essentially, this movie is a variation of the story of King Arthur (the character is named Arthur, in case there's any reason to doubt), in which our hero has to fight to win back his birthright to rule Atlantis and to prevent his half-brother from destroying the surface world. Also, there's a cameo by an octopus playing the drums (how can you not like that?). These movies are based on the DC Comics character, with the title character played by Jason Momoa.

The Curse of La Llorona (2019)
La Llorona (2019)

Yeppers, two movies came out the same year using the theme of the story of La Llorona, so if you're into frightening tales of women doomed for drowning their own children, this was a banner year for you.

Then we have all those underwater adventure stories via TV, of which these are only a few:

Sea Hunt (1958–61)

Lloyd Bridges (father of actors Jeff and Beau Bridges) starred in this television series that gave most average people their first look at scuba diving, since it was so new then. Bridges plays Mike Nelson and he was generally sent to investigate something—a sunken treasure, an abandoned ship, or some sort of political intrigue that made its way to the bottom of the ocean. Every episode has an underwater battle, generally with Nelson fighting another man, a great white shark, or some such critter who thought he looked like dinner. Interesting thing about the episodes—do you think any network would play a 26-minute program in a 30-

minute slot? Ha! But they did in the olden days. If you want to see an ep, you can check out YouTube—they're all there.

Man from Atlantis (1977–78)
Patrick Duffy, Alan Fudge, and Belinda Montgomery starred in this short-lived TV series. Patrick Duffy plays an amnesiac they call Mark Harris. He's amphibious—can breathe underwater and has webbed feet. So naturally, he's recruited to help with whatever needs to be investigated below the surface. Occasionally there's a creature (a genetically engineered jellyfish who wants to eat him— maybe the brother of the jellyfish from *Sphere*) or two, but mostly it's a mad scientist at work. We have fond memories of this.

Flipper! First a movie (1963), then a TV series (1964)
Luke Halpin played a 15-year-old boy, Sandy Ricks, and Mitzi played Flipper. Yes, the male dolphin was played by a girl. Oh, and Chuck Connors played the dad. In the movie, Sandy rescues Flipper after the dolphin had been speared. The two of them become friends during Flipper's recovery, but Sandy's dad made him release the dolphin back into the wild. From then on, adventures continue, often with Flipper saving Sandy or a family member from sharks and other sea critters with sharp teeth. Check out some of the later episodes and you can see he turned out pretty well.

Cecil the Seasick Sea Serpent
Matty's Funday Funnies (1959–62) starred Beanie and Cecil and was later called *Matty's Funnies with Beany and Cecil.* Cecil the Seasick Sea Serpent was loyal to Beanie through thick and thin, but he wasn't all that bright. Children loved him, though. Jacquie was one who wouldn't miss a show. In fact, she had to stop writing this and watch an episode on YouTube: "Beany Meets the Monstrous Monster."

And last but not least, Cthulu

If we're talking sea monsters, we have to mention Cthulu because otherwise there will be a clamor. The creation of HP Lovecraft, Cthulu has been memorable in its various mentions and depictions in media. Lovecraft described the creature thus: "A monster of vaguely anthropoid outline, but with an octopus-like head whose face was a mass of feelers, a scaly, rubbery-looking body, prodigious claws on hind and fore feet, and long, narrow wings behind." If you want to know about Cthulhu (remember, this is Lovecraft's creation, not actual legend), there are videos on YouTube about the world Lovecraft created and Cthulhu's place in it.

Cthulu

Question of the chapter: Can you sing the song to *Flipper*? Bonus question: What's your favorite movie or television show with a water beastie?

Ceremonial Haida sea monster.

Chapter 2
Water Beasties in the Americas

Water beasties are everywhere in the Americas! Let's start in Alaska and head south along the coast.

Alaska!
Nearly all indigenous people in this area have one elemental spirit in common, and it lives in the orca—the killer whale, but known to many indigenous peoples as "Sea Wolf." While stories about the orca vary from culture to culture, nearly all attribute supernatural powers to this awe-inspiring animal.

Other tribes believe that the Sky (or Star) Nation brought Orca to Ina Maka (Mother Earth) from the Dog Star Sirius (the Home of the Ancestors). It was then that this "Great Wolf" was made Keeper of the Ocean, and Guardian of the Cosmic Memory—hence the name "Sea" (for the waters in which She would now dwell) "Wolf" (in remembrance of the Home World whence they came).

Orcas figure into many Native American creation stories, and are often associated with ancestors, wisdom, compassion, and longevity.

There are other water spirits, even a few goddesses: for one, there's the Inuit goddess Sedna, who lives at the bottom of the sea. She has the head and torso of a woman, and the rest is fish. (Mermaid on steroids, basically.) She controls all the animals in the sea, including the orca. There are variations of her origins, but they all seem to have at least one element in common: she has her fingers cut off for one reason or another before she sinks to the bottom of the sea. Make of that what you will. (But this sculpture shown here gives her fingers. She's a goddess, she should be able to regrow fingers if she chooses, right?)

Sedna

Flying—or Swimming—Southward, Thereabouts
The Bokwus is a scary forest spirit found mostly in the deep forests of the Pacific Northwest. If you hear water running where there are no streams or pine cones falling where there's only brush, run! Many hunters or travelers have been lured into streams, then lost their souls to these greedy creatures.

In addition, there is a serpentine creature that has been reported from time to time in the Salish Sea, which is an inland body of water that encompasses the Puget Sound and the waters off of Vancouver, British Columbia. This should come as no surprise, considering this area is also the home of the legendary Sasquatch. The serpent cryptid has been dubbed a cadborosaurus, and as you may expect, more research is required.

And in British Columbia (or thereabouts) is Ogopogo, thought to live in Lake Okanagan in British Canada. First Nations folklore has it that the Ogopogo is a lake creature, a water demon, that for some people is an evil entity that demanded a live sacrifice in order to cross the lake. (Small animals for the most part.) Other peoples viewed the water beastie as a sacred spirit who protects the valley.

In the Northeast, the Abenaki, Penobscot, Maliseet, and Passamaquoddy have the legend of Swamp Woman, who lives in the swamps and wails a mournful song. Some say she lures children to the swamp so she can eat them, but others claim she's mourning the loss of her own child. (Some similarities to the legend of La Llorona, in Central American mythology. Also some horror movies, but that's neither here nor there.)

Then there are Paiutes, who have the water babies who haunt Pyramid Lake. It's said they're the spirits of the deformed babies thrown into the lake as a sacrifice. These water babies are responsible for disappearing fishermen. You don't want to see them. Then there's Iya, who is a Lakota demon who controls rain- and thunderstorms and is a general evildoer.

From the Mi'kmaq (also spelled Micmac) are the Mi'kmaq water faeries, from the Canadian Maritime Provinces around Quebec. Here's a faery legend from the Mi'kmaq people:

A man saw the most beautiful woman he'd ever seen, and he wanted her to be his wife. Eventually, he did marry her and they had a baby. They were happy for a while, but after a time she wanted to visit her home, and he agreed.

Apparently he hadn't asked too many questions, such as "So where are you from?" He quickly learned. They went to the shore, and once there, she walked straight into the lake. At first her husband was afraid to follow, but she persuaded him to go with her under the surface of the water. Soon things began to look very much as they did in the upper world, and after a while they reached a large village in the midst of a beautiful wooded country.

"My father is chief here," the wife explained. And she led her husband to her father's lodge, where they and the child were warmly welcomed. The chief and his wife had the form of fish below the waist and of human beings above the waist—yes, it's the legend of the mermaid, far from where you might think of it.

The Passamaquoddy have a sea monster, too. Apotumk'n is a giant sea serpent with fangs who lives in Passamaquoddy Bay. She lunges from the sea and drags unsuspecting children to their deaths. So kids, don't get too close to the water! She was once a human and still has long red hair, but otherwise has a serpentine appearance. So look out for giant serpent-like creatures with long red hair. It's good to be suspicious!

Then there's the sea monster Mishipizheu, a creature of the Ojibwe who lived on the shores of Lake Superior. Other peoples around the Great Lakes and Mississippi Valley incorporated Mishipizheu into their lore as well. This creature is also known as the Great Horned Lynx and Underwater Panther—it has the scales of a snake, the body of a feline (panther or lynx), the horns of a bison, and spikes on its back. Mishipizheu live in the deepest lakes and rivers, rule the weather, are fearsome, and its breath can bring death. If you were to gussy up this creature with more scales, yes, they'd look just like the usual descriptions of Western dragons. Up in Lake Manitoba we run into Manipogo, a great big snake (specifically, serpentine cryptid), with a lot in common with the Loch Ness monster over in Europe. The monster can be found in an episode of the TV show *Grimm*, "Mishipeshu."

And of course, near Magog Quebec, near Lake Memphremagog (Algonquin meaning "where there is an expanse of water," according to some sources), there's another Nessie-type of creature legend. Sightings of Memphre, as the water beastie is known, go back as far as the 18th century.

Traveling south, we have some classic water beasties, even in areas you don't necessarily connect with water—but you do in the form of, say, rain. According to some sources, Kukulkan is one of the best known yet most mysterious deities of Central America as the main god of the Yucatec Maya, considered to be a variation of Quetzalcoatl, known as the "Plumed Serpent" or the "Feathered Serpent." Other variations of the same water-based beastie are the Huastecs god Ehecati and the Quiché Maya god Gucumatz. Kukulkan also had variations as the War Serpent and the Vision Serpent, as gods of maize and agriculture, and of earthquakes. Some stories had the creature change into a human man and then change back.

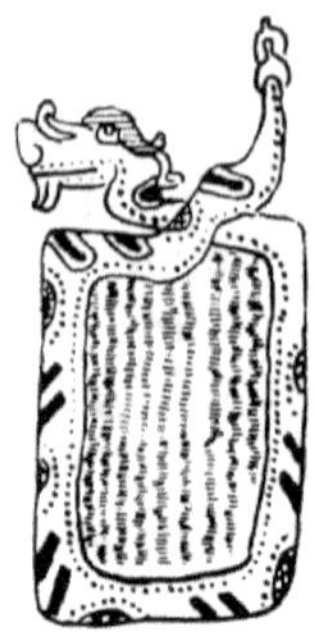

Mayan rain serpent, as found in the Codex Cortes.

Vision serpent.

Quetzalcoatl, or Kukulkan, has been in the pop culture eye as well, in the form of HP Lovecraft's fiction, the TV series *Stargate: SG-1*, *Star Trek*, video games, and more.

La Llorona

The monsters don't have to live in the water, but just hang around in it, doomed to stay, as we'll see in other cultures. In Central America, a story goes that a woman named Maria was madly in love with a man. He wanted her but not her children, so she drowned them. But he refused to be with a woman who'd do such a thing. When she died, the gates of heaven were closed to her and she became the ghost known as La Llorona. She haunts the lakes and rivers of the region, wailing for her children. In some variations of the legend, she actually takes children and drowns them. When we get to Europe, we'll see variations of this same story. (This story was also used in an episode of the TV show *Grimm*, and you can find the horror movies based on the legend too. In fact, if you're interested in myths and legends, check out the show—you should be able to find episodes online.)

Continuing on south to South America, we encounter the munuane, a short guy who's protective of fish and even the local fishermen, as long as they only take what they need, but he gets nasty with people who overfish or otherwise abuse their privileges. He's toothless and has eyes in his knees, and if you annoy him, he will boil you up for a nice soup. So pay attention to fishing etiquette. Also look out for anyone with eyes in their knees.

The coco (or *cuca* for the feminine; also *cucuy*) has dragonish qualities. The coco is also referred to as a "ghost-monster," largely found in Hispanic and Portuguese-based cultures. The creature is described as a female alligator taking humanoid form. The name is derived from the Portuguese *coca*, meaning—yes, that's right, dragon.

But there are also water deities that, although they can be alarming, aren't necessarily monsters. The Aztec water deity Chalchihuitlicue (say that three times fast!) translates as "She of the Jade Skirt" or "She Whose Night-robe of Jewel-stars Whirls Above." Chalchihuitlicue presided over fertility and childbirth, and according to some texts, she created a massive flood, and the only ones who were left standing (so to speak) turned themselves into fishes. Though sometimes she can be seen as a frog, a snake, or a river, most often she's depicted as a woman with a yellow face and wearing a blue coronet with green feathers, carrying a water plant and vase with a cross on the side. In Aztec mythology, the cross represents fertility. When depicted as a river, she has a prickly pear growing from the water, and the fruit of the prickly pear represents a vagina. Or so we've read.

Chalchihuitlicue

The Incas had Paryaqaqa, a god born on the peak of Paryaqaqa Mountain. Nowhere near the ocean, but water-based, nonetheless. Jacquie couldn't find much on him other than if he weren't appeased, he very well might bring floods (more flooding!). On Cochamama, also known as Mother Sea, there wasn't much information, either, but both deities are worth further research.

And one more tidbit

Wikipedia offers a list of water monsters around the world. It's by no means complete because they entirely neglected Sharley, a serpentine monster that allegedly lives in Payette Lake, Idaho. It's said that his name was originally Charley, but then no sober person has ever seen him, so who knows. Some of the lake monsters offered by Wikipedia have already been mentioned, but there are a few that sound interesting. There's Morag in Loch Morar, in Scotland (think of the annual conventions in Scotland when Morag and Nessie get together!); the Lagarfljot Worm in Iceland; Lariosauro in Italy; Nahuelio in Argentina; Muyso in Colombia; the Van Gölü Canavari in Turkey; and Tahoe Tessie in Lake Tahoe and the Flathead Lake Monster, in Montana. Consider any convention in which lake monsters get together. Fun!

Question of the chapter: Do you have a lake/water monster or spirit in your area? If so, tell us about it! Also, of the sea monsters listed here, which one fascinates you most?

Lady of the Lake

Chapter 3
Water Beasties Across Europe and the British Isles

Let's go a-Viking! Hitch up your wagons—be sure to tar 'em up good first to make 'em water-resistant, because we'll have to cross the ocean—and head over to Viking country. In the Scandinavian countries, there's a lot of water beastie and water-based culture. You've probably heard of the will o' the wisp, and up north, they're said to be the ghosts of those who drowned in lakes. They can be hostile or helpful, because there are stories in which they lead a lost living being back to their home but other stories in which they lure the lost to their doom in the water.

Water is a recurrent theme up in the Scandinavian cultures. The draugr (plural "draugar") is the ghost of a man who drowned out in the open sea. He appears as a corpse or in skeletal form covered in seaweed and screams a blood-curdling cry, and he shows up at night during storms at sea, drowning sailors and fishermen and sinking their vessels. If the seafarers spot him, they know he's there to drown them, so they must race to land if possible to thwart him. He's one scary dude, also known as the aptrgangr, which means "after-goer," as in the "one who walks after death."

Did we mention there are both land draugar *and* sea draugar? Yes! Those Norsemen killed and buried at sea sometimes end up as sea draugar, and catching sight of one could be an omen of your own death at sea.

Off the coast of Greenland and in the northern Atlantic, you'd be best steering clear of the kraken, a terrifying squid so large it can be mistaken for an island. If sailors wanted to avoid becoming dinner, they would go out of their way to make sure they were nowhere nearby, but they were still in danger because when the kraken moves, it creates whirlpools that can suck a ship down, ensuring an unwanted visit to Davy Jones's locker.

Other water-based Nordic demons include the Näck, or Nøkk: This is a male water spirit who lured women, especially pregnant women, and young children, to the lake or river by playing the violin. When the victim came too close, they were sucked into the Nøkk's trap and drowned. The Nøkk is a shapeshifter but he's often seen as a naked man sitting in a waterfall. No mention is made of how the violin manages to survive the water. So steer clear of naked men playing a violin in a waterfall. (There is a Japanese spider demon who lures men to their deaths also in a waterfall, which we will go into in a later chapter.)

Another Scandinavian demon associated with water is the Bäckahäst, or brook horse. This is a beautiful white steed that beckons a human to ride him. Once he lures the rider to his back, he plunges into the river or lake and drowns his victim. This is similar to the Scottish kelpie.

Also among the Norse are water-based serpents. Jormungand was the son of Loki, and he was a sea serpent who was so immense, he coiled around entire islands, and in fact is credited with creating the oceans. Because of Jormungand's size and him being a bit on the obnoxious side, Odin took him to Asgard, where he grew even bigger and more obnoxious. When he grew so large that he encircled Midgard, he bit his own tail (so is linked to the Egyptian cyclic serpent, Ouroboros). Jormungand had the distinction of slaying Thor, but at the cost of his own death at Thor's hand.

Among the Baltic cultures, in particular the Finns, Tuonela, like the Hades of Greek myth, is the underground home of the dead, and for the living to travel there involves crossing the river of Tuonela—this won't be the first time crossing the river to reach the land of the dead is referred to. (We look at rivers and how the dead deal with them in our *Ghosts Along the Silk Road*.) The Finnish war god, Iku-Turso, is said to have risen from the sea. The vindictive Lithuanian god, Bangpūtys, is said to have two faces and a beard, holding a fish in his left hand with a rooster sitting on his head. Maybe that danged chicken is what made him so fowl-tempered. (Ahem.)

As we travel south, we reach the British isles, where there are many familiar water spirits and beasties. For one, there's the morgen, a beautiful young woman, a water spirit, who lures men and then drowns them, like the korrigan. You've heard of a variation of this water spirit in the Arthurian legends. Remember Morgan le Fay?

And speaking of the Arthurian legends, there's the Lady of the Lake, whom we know as the keeper of Excalibur. She gave the sword to Arthur and he returned it to her (at least in Thomas Malory's version). Not mentioned in the Arthurian legends is Lorelei, a siren. The stories about her are pretty modern—1800s on—and based on the legend of Lore Ley (murmuring rock). Lorelei, betrayed by her lover, threw herself from the rock and became a siren. If a man hears her song, he'll be lured to his death. We know a variation of this story in the form of Circe, when we travel south.

But we're still in the British isles. If you're in Scotland, don't tangle with the Blue Men of the Minch! They live in underwater caves between the Shiant Islands and Long Island in the Highlands, and are said to be responsible for many a shipwreck. From Wikipedia: "The mythical blue men may have been part of a tribe of 'fallen angels' that split into three; the first became the ground-dwelling fairies, the second evolved to become the sea-inhabiting blue men, and the remainder the Merry Dancers of the Northern Lights in the sky." The legendary creatures are the same size as humans but, as the name implies, blue.

And then there are the selkies. You've all heard about the selkies. Selkie is the Orcadian word for "seal," so actually, they're sort of wereseals, and relatives of merfolk. Lots of love stories involve these shapeshifters (they're a popular theme in fiction), but most don't end happily. Often, in those stories, a human man will steal a female selkie's sealskin and hide it so she can't shift back to a seal, and many tales are based on that premise, all around the world (but not necessarily selkie). Male selkies are said to be so handsome as to be irresistible to women.

You've heard of kelpies, haven't you? Kelpies are shapeshifters found in Scottish lakes, and they are known to be black horses that can shift to look like humans.

Scotland, it turns out, has a bunch of water spirits. One is the water wraith. According to SupernaturalWiki, it is "a spirit thought to preside over the waters" and reportedly can look like elderly women dressed in green. These creatures, notable because they always look as though they are in a bad mood, try to lure travelers into nearby bodies of water. So if you run across crotchety old women hanging out near rivers or lakes, consider avoiding them.

And of course, there are the merpeople: In the legends in Western Europe, they live in kingdoms at the bottom of the ocean. Legends of half-fish and half-human (mostly beautiful women, although there are mermen, too) abound all over, from ancient Babylon's fish gods and the Greek sirens and tritons, to the merpeople of the Europeans. Mermaids lure sailors with their enchanting songs and then take their victims to the underwater kingdom, never to be seen again. We go deeper (so to speak) into the merfolk legends around the world in Chapter 8.

What about dragons? Yes, there are legends of water-based dragons, all over the world. Here, another name for Western dragons is wyrm, an Old English word now evolved to "worm." This term is more commonly used for serpentine, water-dwelling dragons but can be used for any dragon type. Water-dwelling dragons are known to be especially common in Britain. On England's coast southeast of London is a village called Lyminster, and it had a dragon known as the Knucker. The Knucker lived in a bottomless pool that is reputed to have a hoard of treasure at the bottom. (Except if it's bottomless…but who are we to quibble.) This dragon had a taste for maidens (another common thread in Western dragon lore) and had eaten them all, except for the daughter of the King of Sussex. So you can imagine that the king was a little worried. The princess was probably biting her nails, too. Anyway, the king put out word that any knight who slew the dragon would be rewarded with the king's daughter in marriage (with or without chewed fingernails). So of course a knight

did slay the dragon and they all lived happily ever after—
except of course for the maidens who had already been
consumed. There are a few other versions of this story. One
from the Mysterious Beasts site recounts a tale of a "local
lad named Jim Puttock fed the dragon an indigestible
pudding" and poisoned the beast, but accidentally got some
of the dragon's blood on his hand and died when he wiped
his mouth after drinking a pint. So always remember to
wash your hands after poisoning a wicked dragon.

Then there's France, where your health will be better if you
stay away from a Drac. (Of course, this may be the case all
over the world, but in France, they state it explicitly.) These
dragons live underwater, either sea or lake. Gervase of
Tilbury wrote: "They also commonly assert, that the Dracs
assume the human form, and come early into the public
market-place without any one being thereby disturbed.
These, they say, have their abode in the caverns of rivers,
and occasionally, floating along the stream in the form of
gold rings or cups, entice women or boys who are bathing
on the banks of the river; for, while they endeavour to grasp
what they see, they are suddenly seized and dragged down
to the bottom: and this, they say, happens to none more
than to suckling women, who are taken by the Dracs to rear
their unlucky offspring; and sometimes, after they have
spent seven years there, they return to our hemisphere."

And what about the vila? Slavic legend claims they're the
souls of deceased maidens, now spirits of storms and wind.
A vila controls clouds, skies, rivers—some location from
which they control the weather. Not only that, they're
shapeshifters. When in animal form, they're often swans or
horses. When in human form, they're beautiful women with
wings. (Jacquie borrowed some traits from the vila for her
Faery Special Romances.)

We didn't even begin to skim the surface (pardon the pun) of water monster lore in Europe, so if we missed your favorite, please let us know.

Question of the chapter: If you were to create your own water beastie, which combination of the above or others would you pick?

Poseidon and his trident.

Chapter 4
Water Beasties in Slavic, Greek, and Roman Land

The water lore in this region is dark; lots of luring unsuspecting humans to their deaths.

In Slavic lore, a rusalka (plural rusalki) is a ghost of a young woman who died violently, often a suicide or murder, often by drowning. Rusalki are also known to take the form of a water spirit or a mermaid. Lakes and rivers are bodies of water often known to be haunted by the rusalki, so it's best to ask the locals if there are any stories. This particular kind of ghost is not generally hostile, and they will rest quietly if their unjust deaths are avenged. Rusalki are also thought to be those young women who died abrupt and violent deaths without proper funeral rites. (As we walk around the world, you'll find that the proper death ceremonies will do wonders to calm down unquiet spirits, but that's another topic and another book, specifically our book on ghosts. Eilis has given workshops on how important death rituals are!)

Much like the Greek sirens and the legend of Lorelei of Western Europe, the rusalki are beautiful women of the lakes whose songs lure men to their deaths by drowning. These are malevolent spirits, to be feared by all men. But even rusalki aren't bad all the time, and they can finally rest if their deaths are avenged.

While the water version of the rusalki are quiet if their deaths are avenged, there's the vodianoi. This Slavic water demon is particularly vicious, so watch out around any body of water, be it river, lake, or the smallest stream. This demon, which can shapeshift into a fish, has a sole purpose, and it is to drown those who dare enter his waters. Vodianoi are the spirits of those men who, like the rusalki, have met violent deaths, but there's no guarantee that they'll simmer down once their deaths are avenged. Only millers and fishermen are safe from the vodianoi—millers because in earlier times they sacrificed a person to the vodianoi each year, and fishermen because they traditionally gave the vodianoi the first of their catch. All others are in peril around these demons.

Then there's the Greek underworld, which could only be reached by crossing one of the rivers of the dead; the rivers Styx and Acheron were those that the newly dead were ferried across by the boatman Charon. There are rivers of the dead all over the world, as it turns out.

Greece is the heart of Western civilization, and if you take a look at the map, where the country is situated also explains why it has in turn influenced and been influenced by its neighboring cultures. Who's not familiar with the Greek gods and goddesses, after all, and the Greek nature spirits— faeries by nature, if not by name? There are naiads (water spirits ruling lakes, rivers, springs, and fountains) and nereids (sea spirits).

There's also a water dragon of sorts in Greek legends. The Trojan Cetus, or Ceto, was often equated with Python (known as the rotting one), a dragon born of the fetid slime left behind by the great Deluge. Others call her the Tartarean lamprey, and assigned her to the dark, swampy pit of Tartarus. This makes Cetus a daughter of monstrous sea-gods, and presumably links her with rotting sea-scum and fetid salt-marshes. In all cases, she was described as the consort of Typheus, a monstrous storm-demon who challenged Zeus.

Then there are the Phorcydes, who were the children of the sea god Phorcys and Cetus and include the Hesperides, the Graeae, the Gorgons (see below), Scylla (said to be the daughter of Hecate and Phorcys and associated with the world), Charybdis, and other nymphs and monsters, mostly associated with the sea. (Charybdis was mentioned in our chapter about Hollywood.) "The sea monster Charybdis was believed to live under a small rock on one side of a narrow channel," according to Wikipedia.

Scylla was another sea-monster, but this one lived within a much larger rock. Because they lived across from each other, the challenge for sailors was to sail between them, inviting disaster. Charybdis created gigantic whirlpools, while Scylla was "transformed … by the sorceress Circe or Poseidon's consort, the sea nymph Amphitrite, into a monster with six legs and six heads, each with lot of teeth." Amphitrite, the consort of Poseidon, is also noted as the mother of Triton, the guy with the conch (see the end of this chapter).

We all know the mortal Gorgon, Medusa (the one with the snakes as hair and gets annoyed when nobody will look her in the eye). Her sisters (Euryale and Sthenno) and brother (Nanas) have similar appearances: snakes for hair, brass hands, scales, and fangs—also sometimes depicted with beards. Turns out that Euryale and Sthenno are queens of the underworld and can go anywhere—land or sea, favoring the sea. Medusa herself, however, is noted more for her stone-causing visage than her relatives.

The hippocampus, front part horse and the back part fish, served Poseidon. They're benevolent water beasties, good for a change up in your stories. And handy, since your hero can ride one. They made a movie appearance in *Percy Jackson*. They're also known as sea horses.

Hippocampus, everyone's favorite sea horse. Poseidon was often depicted as riding on one. Note the front is horse-like and the back is fish-like.

And finally, mention should be made of Triton, the son of Poseidon and Amphitrite. He had the upper torso of a man and lower half of a fish. But he's not a merman, although he's sometimes referred to as such (*The Little Mermaid*, DC Comics' *Wonder Woman* and *Aquaman,* to mention a few). Triton carries a trident like his daddy, and also a twisted conch, which he blows like a bugle to control the ocean waves.

Triton, son of Poseidon and Amphitrite, with his trusty conch. Note the family resemblance to daddy Poseidon.

Question of the chapter: If you had a hippocampus, would you feed it hay or seaweed?

Enki, the Mesopotamian god of freshwater oceans.

Chapter 5
Wet Africa and Across the Middle East

There are water myths and legends even in the driest of climates, in the form of rivers and lakes and nearby (but not that nearby) seas. The water beasties we encounter by the time we get down past the Mediterranean Sea have less and less in common with European culture, and taking a step to Africa, we find a continent both wet and dry. It's a big place, filled with mystery of all kinds. That includes water-based ones.

There are water myths and legends along ethnic groups on the continent, among which are the Cameroonian Sawa's jengu, gap-toothed water spirits with long, woolly hair living in the rivers and the nearby sea. The jengu acted as a medium between the living and the dead and could cure disease, and they played an important role in some rituals. Elsewhere in Africa are the mami wata, another water spirit similar to the jengu.

One of the marvelous things about exploring the myths and legends of Africa is that because it's such a big place with so many different cultures ranging from north to south, and to a great extent not fully explored (and ancient!), the myths we run across might not be myths at all. One example is the stories about the inkanyamba, a gigantic eel that pops up in the tales among the Zulu and the !Xhosa. Some say the creatures control the weather. But there are freshwater eels that get as long as six feet long, so who knows? Maybe there are inkanyamba after all.

There's a variety of water deities and spirits you can find mention of in central Africa, among which are Nommos in Dogon, which according to Wikipedia are "amphibious spirits that are worshipped as ancestors"; and Mindis, a female protector of the Fatick region who appears in the form of a manatee (those manatees again!). In Yoruba there are orisha, a river version (Oshun) and an ocean version (Olokun), and Yemoja, who is both a river and an ocean orisha. Nyami Nyami is a river spirit who can be found in Zambia and Zimbabwe. In Congo, there are a slew of water deities and spirits, some of which may sound familiar. There's Bunzi, the goddess of rain; Funza, the goddess of waters; Kalunga, who is the god of death and the border between the living and the world of the dead; Kimbazi, the goddess of sea storms; and Kuitikuiti, the serpent god of the Congo river.

And speaking of Congo, what about the kongamato in the cultures around Zambia, Angola, and Congo? A winged creature but without feathers said to live in the rivers and swamps in the region, the kongamato's descriptions match those of the fossil records of the dinosaurs in the region. Again, might be a myth, might not be.

Then up in Liberia there's the gbahali, which by its description sounds like a crocodile. Not out of the question, right? It gets to be as large as 30 feet long, they say. (Compare this with crocodilian myths as dragons in the South Pacific, so anything's possible!) Apparently there was a creature called the *Postosuchus*, now extinct, and its fossil remains match those of the gbahali. So this might be just like the case of the deep-sea fish coelacanth that we mentioned right at the beginning.

And what about the ninki nanka, which is said to live in the rivers in the Gambian area? It's said to have a body of a crocodile, the head of a horse (with horns, so it's sort of like a rhino), and a neck like a giraffe, and said to be 50 feet long. No fossil record on this one, so we can only assume it's a myth. Maybe. Maybe we just haven't explored enough and haven't found the fossil remains yet.

Then there's the grootslang, meaning "great snake" in Afrikaans. This too is supposed to get up there in length, a whole 60 feet, sticking close to the rivers and lakes in the southern part of the continent. They grow 'em big in Africa, it seems (maybe). It's a big, mysterious continent, as you can tell, full of myths and legends. More research is required.

Once we head east to arrive in the Middle East, known for its aridity (erroneous, since there are lots of oases, watery, verdant areas—think of the cedars of Lebanon, which would need water, right?), we have myths and legends of antiquity, and that includes lots and lots of water references.

How far back does that go? There's the ancient story of Gilgamesh, perhaps the oldest tale still in existence (as far back as 5,000 years), in which ol' Gil runs into a river ferryman (yes, again!) whom he persuades to take him across the waters of death. Water being synonymous with death particularly in the form of a river is common imagery around the world, and Gilgamesh's encounter with a ferryman is one of the earliest stories involving it. (That ferryman, if you'll recall your European water myths, shows up a lot, too, and also as we head into Asia.)

Statue of Gilgamesh.

Then there's Abzu, the water lord in Sumerian mythology who threatens to take back the creation of man by use of a flood, but then he is imprisoned beneath the earth by the Mesopotamian god Enki, also referred to as Ea. Enki rules the freshwater ocean of groundwater and is shown with fish scales, with two streams of water pouring off his shoulders (one the Tigris River, the other the Euphrates). Then there's his wife, Ninhursag, who is the goddess of the waters.

Mesopotamian gods include Enbilulu, the god of rivers and canals; Nammu, the goddess of the primeval sea, Nanshe, she who presides over the Persian Gulf and fishing, among other matters, and Sirsir, the god of mariners. Those readers who have read *Dragons Along the Silk Road* may remember the name Tiamat, who here is known as the goddess of saltwater, as well as the mother of all gods.

And of course there's the fertility goddess Astarte, known by so many names in the region—Derceto, Dea Syriae, Ishtar, Atargatis. As Atargatis, she is the chief goddess of northern Syria, described as a goddess connected to the sea since she was identified as a goddess with the body of a fish.

The reverse of a coin of Demetrius III depicts fish-bodied Atargatis.

The Egyptians had Anuket, goddess of the Nile, and Khnum, god of the Nile; and Bairthy, goddess of water; Hapi, god of the annual flooding of the Nile (yes, the Nile River is and was important to local culture), and Satet, the goddess of the Nile's floods. There was also Nephthys, who was the goddess of rivers, death, mourning, the dead, as well as the night. Sobek was also god of the Nile, but was shown as a crocodile or a man with the head of a croc. And of course, who doesn't know Osiris, god of the dead and afterlife, but who was first known as a god of water?

Not only that, we have references to the "sea-monster" or "pole serpent" in the Bible, the leviathan of the stories from Canaan of old, symbolic of chaos. (I found a reference that in modern Hebrew, "leviathan" apparently means "whale.") Some religions in the region viewed the leviathan as a demon in the shape of a whale with seven heads, seen as the king of lies. Ruling the leviathan is Yah, the god of the waters in Canaanite myths.

The Abrahamic story of crossing the river Jordan to reach the promised land is a variation of those that we encounter all around the world (the Gilgamesh myth, remember? And Tuonela up in Finland too, and in Asia), since we also run into the concept of crossing a river in order to reach the land of the dead in other cultures. Water is important, no matter the form. It's always the crossing that makes the difference, so the river itself is the demarcation between life and death. See our previous chapter about the Greek myths referring to the various rivers of the dead, including the Acheron (known as the river of woe), the Cocytus (the river of lamentation), the Phlehethon (the river of fire), the Lethe (the river of forgetfulness), and the Styx (the river of hate).

Then there are the flood stories!
The story of the great flood has many variations in many cultures all over the world, not just in the Middle East (there's the story of a great flood in Hindu mythology, for instance, and we've already referenced reports of a great Deluge wherever we go), and in the flood myths of various Near East countries, the flood survivor is given different names and twists. In the Sumerian myth, for example, the flood survivor is saved by the god Enki. Flood myths are often studied alongside creation myths, in which the floods occur so that humanity, always corrupted by that point, can experience rebirth. Those myths—Mesopotamian, Hindu, Greek, Mesoamerican, South American, so they pop up all over—all have a local mythical figure who works to save the local culture from complete destruction. (The epic of Gilgamesh includes such a story. Noah is the one you may be most familiar with.)

Working our way across the desert, we eventually get to Persia, and according to Zoroastrianism, Ahura Mazda created seven archangels, and each was responsible for a particular specialty. Apam Napat is the god of water, and Ardvi Sura Anahita is the goddess of all the waters of the earth and the source of the cosmic ocean. She is regarded as the source of all life, and the work *Aban Yasht* is dedicated to her. Then there was Haurvatat, who was responsible for perfection and plenty, as well as being the guardian of water.

And with that, let's find one of the many rivers in the region that lead us from the Iranian peninsula to Afghanistan and beyond to India.

Question of the chapter: What do you think the myths in African cultures have in common with those in the Middle East and Near East?

Saraswati is the goddess of knowledge, but she was also the goddess of rivers before she resigned. She is known as Benzaiten in Japan, often shown as playing a biwa, a musical instrument, as she is the goddess of music, knowledge, and water.

Chapter 6
The Water Beasties of the Far East

Once we arrive in the Far East, the water myths and legends are both familiar and different. There's a great flood, of course, because there's always one mentioned everywhere, but it's not quite the one you have in mind.

Water is everywhere and so are the water beasties in the Far East. The place is, as you may have noticed, also a very big place and encompasses a good many different waters and attendant myths. Let's start with India, which is a subcontinent and has a lot of water in it and surrounding it.

Here's a theme you may find familiar by now: As we approach the Indian subcontinent, when we start to examine Hindu mythology, we find the river Vaitaran, which marks the boundary between the living and the dead. In Hindu tradition, there are places along that river that make it easier for the newly deceased to cross into the underworld. (This detail, about a place along the river between the living and the dead where it's easier to make the crossing, comes up elsewhere, in fact later in this chapter in Japanese lore.) There's that thing about rivers and the deceased again! (But the naiads—the river spirits— in Greek myth aren't particularly deadly, so take that as you will.)

In Hindu myth, Manu was a man who survived a great flood. (Yes, that thing about a great flood again.) Here's the story: One day when Manu was at the river, a fish swam into his hands and begged him to save its life. It turned out to be the god Matsya in disguise. Manu did so, and the fish warned him that soon a great flood would destroy all life. So Manu built a boat and was towed to a mountaintop by Matsya, who had turned into a big fish. And in that way, Manu survived the flood. Is the story vaguely familiar to you?

Saraswati is the goddess of knowledge, but she was also the goddess of rivers. Varun is the god of rain and the ocean above the heavens, while Yami, sister to the god of death and daughter of the sun god, became the goddess of rivers after Saraswati resigned from the position. (Considering Hindu mythology also has Ganesha, often considered to be the god of bureaucracy, the idea that a god can resign from a position should not be a surprise. That god is also the protector of authors, so keep that in mind.)

And you want familiar stories? There are also stories about legendary cities swallowed by the sea, sometimes flourishing underwater, sometimes not. According to legend, Krishna ruled over the city of Dwarka until it was swallowed by the sea. Stories abound about it. For Hindus, finding that city would be like finding the Holy Grail. Of course, those stories about the lost city might be at an end, because in recent years there have been reports of marine archaeologists having discovered a sunken city off the shores of southeast India. Stone reliefs excavated seem to show that it may be indeed Dwarka, perhaps 12,000 years old. This is like discovering Atlantis, so once more, we really don't know what lies beneath the waters!

And of course, there's the aquatic version of a familiar mythological beast, the dragon. As opposed to the dragon legends of the West, where the dragons mentioned are almost always winged and mostly sticking to dry land, the dragons of the Far Eastern cultures are usually water-based, associated with rainfall and bodies of water as well as fertility, usually wingless, and serpentine. Varuna, the Hindu god of storms, is regarded as the king of the naga, the local version of the dragon. Paradoxically, the naga is viewed as the personification of drought.

Varuna, the Hindu god of storms.

And then in China, there's the yu, a turtle-like demon that lurks in shallow waters around lakes and rivers and attacks humans by spitting sand at them. Very rude! The opponent of water beasties in Chinese culture is the ba, the demon that can cause droughts. Then there's the wu zhiqi, a water demon in the vague form of an ape with a head of white fur and a green body, known to be as strong as nine elephants. And that's just a drop in the bucket (sorry). Between China and India you're going to find endless numbers of water spirits, with small variations depending on what region you find yourself in. A good number of them are malevolent, come to think of it, so step carefully around those puddles.

Back to dragons. Dragons play an important role in Chinese myth, often bound to the elements. Panlong are specifically the water dragons, believed to inhabit the waters of all Asia (the Near, Middle and Far East, so ALL of Asia). In Chinese myth, the dragon has expanded abilities and can disguise itself, fly, form into clouds, and (of course) turn into water.

Dragons are tightly connected with the waters of China. There are four dragon kings according to Chinese legend, each representing one of the known seas in traditional Chinese culture—again, the connection with water, including weather. In fact, the king of Wu-Yue was referred to as the "Sea Dragon King" because of his work in bringing water to his people.

Dragon kings were believed to consist of four separate dragons, each of which ruled over one of the four seas in the north, east, south, and west. These dragon kings could shapeshift into human form, and were believed to live in crystal palaces guarded by shrimp and crabs.

You'll find any number of variations of water deities in China that are echoed in Asian locales. There's the Gonggong, a dragon water god with the head of a human who is responsible for great floods when he's angered (so don't); and there's Mazu, who is the goddess of the sea and the protector of sailors. Rivers have their own deities, including Ehuang and Nuying, goddesses who protect the Xiang River, and Hebo, who is the god of the Yellow River. Tam Kung is a sea deity specifically worshipped in Hong

Kong and Macau who can forecast the weather. Finally, there are the Kings of the Water Mortals.

Just a few steps over from China, following a river or two, we get to Korea, where the legends speak of imoogi—enormous pythons believed to be juvenile dragons that lived in water or caves and had to survive for a thousand years before they could ascend and become true, fully formed dragons. Stories differ on how the imoogi can become full-fledged dragons, whether by surviving a thousand years or by catching a yeouiju, a magical object, that fell from the heavens. Some stories say that the imoogi were cursed and thus can never become dragons. And you have to appreciate King Munmu, who wished to become a dragon upon his death to protect Korea from the Sea of Japan.

Speaking of the Sea of Japan, sailing across it we have the Japanese archipelago. The Ainu, the aboriginal culture of the Japanese islands who live in the far north, have Amemasu, recognized to be the monster who dwells in their lakes, and they have Repun Kamui, the god of the sea, a reference to the orca.

There are numerous sea, river, and lake beasties in Japanese folktales (Japan being a series of islands surrounded by water, so…), and since demons can be both good and evil in Asian myths, it can be tricky to navigate those waters (so to speak). For one, there's the spider demon, the jorogumo, which hangs out near waterfalls, where the creature changes into a beautiful woman who tries to persuade unsuspecting men to marry her. Not a sucker? No problemo! For those who won't fall for that trick, the jorogumo changes into a young woman with a baby (which actually may be the spider demon's eggsack) and asks for help from those men who weren't interested in being seduced—at which point she binds the legs of her prey with her webbing and drowns him. Moral of the story? If you meet up with a beautiful woman at any waterfall, avoid her. You just don't know. Also, men are dupes. (We ran across a variation of why you should stay away from people at waterfalls in Europe, but in that case, it was a naked man playing the violin. Dunno about you, but Eilis is going to start looking at waterfalls suspiciously.)

And have you heard about the kappa? The kappa are Japanese water demons, sly, slippery monkey-like creatures, greenish and almost human looking with green seaweed hair, with long noses and an indentation on top of their saucer-shaped heads, with a sly look in their green eyes. That indentation holds water, and it must always hold water for the kappa's continued existence and powers. If a human tricks them so the water falls out, the kappa loses its powers. The kappa can be found near rivers and ponds, looking to trap humans and in particular children to drown them, feeding on their blood, so keep an eye out. If you see someone looking strange and with a greenish complexion…run! In fact, between the jorogumo and the kappa, bodies of water can be the source of a lot of watery demonic activity in Japan. Oh, and kappa are very fond of cucumbers. So if you're planning on having a picnic next to a river or a pond with your bushels of cucumber sandwiches, keep an eye out, because they'll try to drown you *and* steal your cucumbers! (Fun fact: This is why when you go out for sushi, you ask for "kappamaki" to get cucumber rolls. But again, eat them away from bodies of water, just in case.)

Kappa

The dragons of Japan are a lot like the Chinese dragons in appearance, but not identical; they are both water gods, connected with rainfall and lakes and rivers and fertility.

Some other water beasties hanging out around Japanese lore: The wani was a sea monster, according to the historical texts, which translates as descriptions of shark and crocodile, so while there aren't any crocs in Japan, clearly the locals must have known about them from more southern countries and incorporated them into the local legends and myths.

Then there's the giant catfish that lives under the sea. Catfish have alarming visages as it is, so a giant one? Terrifying!

In the ancient, classical Japanese work known as Kojiki, there's an eight-headed and eight-tailed water dragon bested by Susanoo, the god of wind and sea. Then there's Ryujin, the sea god or dragon god, who lives in a palace under the sea, where he keeps gems that can control the tides. The Japanese version of the Hindu goddess Saraswati is Benzaiten, who is the goddess of the sea and water, as well as wealth and luck, with dragons and serpents her messengers and avatars.

In Japan, water—seas, rivers, lakes, oceans—is crucial to the cultural mythology. A famous Buddhist temple in Tokyo, Senso-ji, was founded when a golden statuette of Kannon, the goddess of mercy (parallel to and most likely derived from the Chinese goddess of mercy, Kwan Yin), was found nearby in the Edo River, and the temple was built around the statuette to hide it away from humans, and somewhere in there golden dragons appeared and made their way up into the heavens. But not water dragons, interestingly enough.

Japanese folktales show the water-based culture, including the story of a boy named Taro, who rides on the back of a magical giant turtle and swims to a land under the sea, where he meets the emperor and empress of the seas and finally, after enjoying himself with wonderful food and dance and folks and being showered with rare and exquisite gems, he decides to go back to the land up above…only to find that hundreds of years have passed during his absence, and nothing remains of the life he had. (The moral of the story, of course, is if you get a chance to ride a magical talking turtle who invites you to the world under the sea, think twice.) (Is this a familiar theme? You probably have one much like it in folklore closer to your home. If nothing else, if you're an American, think of the thoroughly land-based story of Rip Van Winkle.)

Then there's nure-onna (literally "wet woman"), who's got the head of a woman and the body of a snake. Despite the stories claiming that she eats people, she's not particularly villainous nor deadly (except for the eating people part).

Nure-onna. Maybe not villainous, but we'll stay away anyway.

And remember the stories wherever you go about a river being the division between life and death? Of course you remember. Here it is again. In the northern region of Japan, there's the Sanzu River, where the newly dead make their way to the afterlife. Known as the river of three crossings, this body of water marks the place between life and death, and the relative difficulty in getting across it and getting to the land of the dead depends on how the soul acted during life. (You can think of the difficulty in crossing to be a version of Purgatory, actually.) Every time Eilis finds out about three rivers that meet in one place, she wonders if that's the way to the afterlife. And decides she doesn't want to find out, not really.

Finally, there's the Dragon's Triangle, also known as the Devil's Sea, an area of ocean about 60 miles or so south of Tokyo. This region seems to be very big or quite small, depending on where you read about it, and it's very much the local equivalent of the Bermuda Triangle. Over the years, fishing boats, pleasure cruises, and more have been lost in the region. Those disappearances could be connected to the underwater eruptions of the volcanoes still active in the Japanese archipelago. Or maybe not. Dragons, maybe (at least that's one theory).

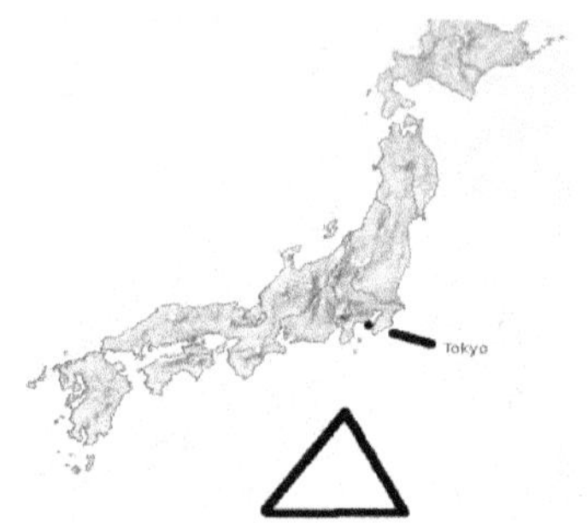

Dragon's Triangle, as done up by Eilis Flynn.

There's also the Formosa Triangle, which is a five-million-square kilometer region in the Pacific where ships also disappear under odd conditions. This triangle is located between Taiwan, Wake Island, and the Gilbert Islands. Eilis hasn't found any reasonable explanation for why, except dragons (again) and vortices. Sort of makes you nervous, doesn't it?

Heading south, starting to explore the vastness of the Pacific, you're going to realize that water truly *is* everywhere (and needs to be, of course). Naga—the dragon/serpent of elsewhere in Asia—are water beasties, truly. In Laotian legends the naga are often shown as water serpents with beaks. In Thailand, the water dragon, which is known as the phaya naga, is regarded as a holy creature.

Cambodian myths also have the naga in their culture, with stories about an ancient empire hidden in a lake and a kingdom in a nearby part of the ocean.

The Mekong River and the legend of the naga are part and parcel of the Thai and Laotian mythologies. The naga rule the river, and annual sacrifices are still held for them, because locals believe that the naga can protect them from danger. There is a yearly sighting in which fireballs seem to rise from the Mekong. The naga sightings seen during this period, of a 60-foot serpent with black-green scales, could be based on a local giant snake indigenous to the area. That's in contrast to the Vietnamese dragon, which is an ever-changing combination of crocodile, snake, lizard, and bird, but still very much a water beastie, only seen near the Mekong and other large bodies of water.

Some well-known naga in the region include Karkotaka, who controls the weather; and Padmavati, the naga queen.

Then there's the colossal squid that was discovered not too long ago in the Southern Ocean. It's estimated to be about forty-six feet long and its beak and eyes are bigger than those of a giant squid. But what really sets it apart from other squids is that in addition to suckers, its limbs are lined with hooks, some that swivel and others that have three points. Now that could do some damage. The big difference is, of course, is that the description makes it sound unreal and downright fantastic. But it's real! (Go back and read the description of Cthulu and know that its creator, H.P. Lovecraft, read widely and had a vivid imagination.)

Question of the chapter: What kind of water-based myths can you think of that could logically be based on reality, just a little distorted?

Bakunawa or giant catfish?

Chapter 7
The Water Beasties of the Pacific Rim

And we finally paddle into the Hawaiian islands and the Pacific region. The shapeshifting sharks of the South Pacific come up a lot in these local stories. But the weresharks aren't malevolent for the most part (despite being weresharks). Some of the stories have the recipients having been victims of drowning at sea or being adopted by a shark god. These sharkshifters can be identified with patterns on their skin that look like tattoos.

The shark king, also known as the shark god, protects the locals and the sea around the islands, but the stories say the shark god fell in love with a human woman, and she bore him a child, a son, who was clearly half-man, half-shark, with a large gaping hole in the middle of his back that looks like a fish mouth. He had many abilities that would protect the people, but because he was so different, he was never accepted, and finally, the locals beat him to death out of fear.

In Polynesian mythology, there's a folktale of a boy named Tahoratakarar who they say was raised by the seas themselves as one of their own. His mother, Takua, was abducted by two evil spirits, and they stole the male baby within her before the sea rose and rescued the infant, and forced the evil spirits into a cloud. Other sea spirits built a big boat for the infant that also acted as a soul collector, sailing at night and searching for anyone who had died at sea. The boat was known as the boat of souls, or the boat of the dead. (Is this a familiar-sounding story? Think of the tale of Charon in Greek myths.)

Not only that, there are the various forms of hantu—spirits—in the Pacific Rim. There's the hantu air, which are water spirits that live in rivers or large lakes, often ghosts of those who have drowned on those bodies of water. They have been known to take on the appearance of a floating log to trick unsuspecting travelers to drown them or eat them. (Check out the Scandinavian water ghosts with similar stories.) Then there are the hantu laut, the sea spirits that are sympathetic to fishermen and sailors and help them in their time of need.

The bakunawa, described as a water dragon in the Philippines with a mouth the size of a lake, a red tongue, whiskers and gills, and not one but two sets of wings (quick, what does a catfish look like?), rose from the ocean and ate the moon to punish the people for killing his sister the sea turtle, and they had to make a lot of noise to make the dragon throw up the moon. The stories also say that the dragons disappeared afterward, so take that as you will.

Bunyip literally means devil, or spirit. It is a mythological creature from Aboriginal Australia, with flippers, a horse-like tail, and walrus-like tusks, said to lurk in swamps, creeks, riverbeds and waterholes. Aborigines, who thought they could hear their cries at night, believed bunyip took humans, mostly women, as a food source when their stock was disturbed, and they tended to blame the bunyip for disease spread around the rivers.

Then there's the story of Tiddalik the frog (sometimes known as Molok), from Australian Aboriginal mythology. In this tale, the frog developed an unexplainable, unquenchable thirst, and drank and drank until all the fresh water that could be found had been drunk, causing animals and plant life everywhere to die. Understandably, there was much resentment, and the other (very thirsty) creatures worked together to get the water back from Tiddalik (by making him laugh, believe it or not). The plan worked, and the water refilled the lakes, the swamps, and the rivers.

Question of the chapter: Name a European water tale that sounds a bit like what you've just read. Can we truly say that the world is connected?

The Little Mermaid statue in Copenhagen

Chapter 8
Mermaids All Around the World, and Selkies Too

Sea cows and manatees are the usual excuse for sailors' ravings about their visions of beautiful (or handsome, depending on who's doing the ranting) half-human, half-fish creatures, luring people to their doom, but here's the thing. Cultures all over the world seem to have similar stories about human–fish hybrid creatures, both alluring and terrifying, and that's enough of an excuse to look into those merfolk stories, right? Deserving of its own chapter, Eilis figured. So she decided to look into the legends and find out what there is to find out. And there's a lot!

From the Disney version (*The Little Mermaid*) to the Asian versions (with little in common with the cute redhead from Disney), you can find mermaids and merfolk in general all over the place. Sometimes they're luring sailors to their doom, sometimes they're aiding hapless humans lost at sea, sometimes they're probably wondering what the heck those land people are doing, but no matter what, there are many, many stories about merfolk, in many variations. It's safe to say that both sides are fascinated by the other (and wondering what the heck the other is doing).

We've already mentioned a few well-known movies (shockingly, *Splash!* was not on our list originally when we put it together), but there is a wealth of merpeople.

Sedna, the Inuit goddess of the sea whom we mentioned in an earlier chapter, can theoretically be put here too; take a look at the image on page 21—she looks like she's part human, part fish, doesn't she? She is reminiscent of a drawing of ningyo-no-zu-Bunka, the Japanese mermaid, which is the face of a human and the rest of a fish. Certainly a contrast to Disney's Ariel.

Stories about merfolk are old, as far back as Mesopotamia and Babylon. There's an Assyrian tale in which the sea goddess Atargatis turns herself into a mermaid to punish herself for "accidentally killing her human lover," according to Wikipedia. Atargatis is shown as both with a human head with fish body and as a fish with a human head, forget the body, which is all fish.

Not only that, there were stories from Greek myths, in this case the Sirens, sometimes depicted as bird-like, sometimes fish-like, in either case luring men to their doom with their song.

Later, the philosopher Pliny the Elder noted that there were reports of mermaids all over the shores of what was Gaul, and that their half-fish bodies, covered with scales, washed up onto the beaches frequently. No speculation noted why.

Even in stories like those from *One Thousand and One Nights*, there were mentions of the people who live in the sea, only different in that they can live on land and under the water, and they can have children who can live underwater (check out Namor and Aquaman, in Chapter 9 about aquatic superheroes—both half-human, half-Atlantean).

Then there are the mermaid stories in British folklore and Western Europe, from that region's earliest times. Around this region, mermaids were considered to be unlucky, portents of disaster. They are symbols of bad weather, much like the red skies at dawn.

Mermaids could be both good and bad; in one Scottish story, the laird of the area was stopped by his servant from jumping into the lake to save a drowning woman, who was actually a mermaid out to drown him (why? He had offended her). But mermaids could also be kind; they were also described to reveal cures for some human diseases. (In Scottish myths, a freshwater mermaid is known as a ceasg, and often cranky. Eilis couldn't find much research to differentiate between freshwater and saltwater merfolk.)

Manx mermaids (as in from the Isle of Man), known as ben-varrey, are known to be more favorable toward humans than elsewhere in the Western world (as opposed to those ceagh in Scotland, who are definitely not).

Irish merfolk, noted to be of endearing disposition (as opposed to Scottish merfolk), are referred to as merrow, and they have a cap that allows them to travel between water and land. There's a story from the 19th century, "Lady of Gollerus," where a green-haired merrow marries a man who steals her cap to keep her from going back to the sea. There are similar stories around the world in which men fall in love with mythical creatures who hold magical items and steal said items to prevent the creatures from leaving.

These mermaids were reported to entice men to the sea, but instead of taking them to their doom, the men were said to live there with the merfolk. Once again, there are variations of this story all over the world.

Then there are selkies, of course. We mentioned them in an earlier chapter. Not quite merfolk but certainly a relative, the selkie, also known as a shapeshifter and popping up frequently in Irish, Scottish, and Icelandic folklore, is known to have a cap of sorts of her own. (We dive deeper into selkies in *Shapeshifters Along the Silk Road*.)

In Irish folktales there's a story about a human female turned mermaid who is later sanctified—a familiar echo to the story of Zennor, just a hop across the water to Cornwall.

The Cornish legend about the village of Zennor, to which a mermaid came to listen to the singing of a man. They fell in love, and they went to live in a nearby cove, where they could be heard singing together on warm summer nights. (The merrow of Ireland are also said to have similar musical leanings.) This story is commemorated in a church there, where there is a chair, estimated to be about six hundred years old, that is decorated with a mermaid carving. In this legend, the mermaid also becomes a saint (Saint Senara, in case you're interested in doing your own deep dive into the topic). This story has inspired modern variations, including Sue Monk Kidd's *The Mermaid Chair*.

This is an interesting contrast to Hans Christian Andersen's fairy tale, whose mermaid suffers because she has no soul. The statue of his Little Mermaid has been a landmark in Copenhagen, Andersen's home, since 1913, with copies all around the world. His version of merfolk inspired others, including those of Oscar Wilde, H.G. Wells, and in more modern times, Claudia Grossman.

Elsewhere in Western Europe, there's the story of Melusine, a freshwater mermaid (sort of). Sometimes depicted with two fish tails or with the lower body of a serpent, perhaps as famous as the Andersen mermaid, mainly because the coffee chain Starbucks has as its symbol a melusine (the logo image is also known as a siren).

Eastern Europe

Merfolk can also be found in other parts of Europe. The Slavic term *rusalka* has different meanings depending on where you go, but basically (as we noted in *Ghosts Along the Silk Road*), they're the spirits of women who've died a violent death and never got the proper burial rites and have become water beasties, with pale greenish hair and pale skin, hanging around the rivers and lakes. This version of rusalka is most often seen in the Slavic states and the Baltic states.

And there are those Greek myths (we couldn't leave the region without something about Greek myths, right?). There are the nereids, the naiads, the oceanids, and of course, the Sirens. But you know about those!

A southerly swim across the Mediterranean gets us to the African continent, where the local myths made their way to the Caribbean and North and South Americas. Mostly female, sometimes male, these folk are usually not friendly toward humans. Then there are the njuzu in Zimbabwe; these mermaids, mostly found in rivers and lakes, can be friendly as well as malevolent toward people. In recent years (2012, to be precise), work on reservoirs came to a halt in Zimbabwe when workers reported that mermaids had chased them away from the construction site.

You don't expect mermaid stories out of Israel, but in 2009, there were reports of a mermaid leaping out of Haifa Bay!

Heading east, there aren't as many myths about merfolk, but there's a Persian term, *maneli*, which means "mermaid." So clearly more research is required. And then we keep going east, toward Asia.

The Asian merfolk

There are the merpeople of Asia, where there are stories about them from all the way back to the fourth-century BCE. There are the early Chinese myths about the shark people, with tears of pearls, and then there are the stories, including one about a man who finds a woman whose hands and feet are webbed and falls in love with her.

Then there are the stories from Korea, where the mermaids are very humanlike. There are tales about the mayor of a town rescuing four mermaids from captivity, and a singing mermaid who warned fishermen of coming storms. The locals thought she was a goddess of the sea and she knew the weather. In addition, there's a story about a fisherman who keeps mermaids as hostages, which inspired a well-regarded movie.

And right across the Sea of Japan is, well, Japan, with merfolk called ningyo-no-zu-bunka, part human but no clear gender. Ningyo don't sound like those western mermaids at all, with a woman's head on a fishy body. Not only that, there are golden horns, a red belly, three eyes on each side of its torso, and a fishy tail end!

Ningyo-no-zu-bunka

We swim (or sail) due south and we find loads more merfolk myths and legends in other parts of the Pacific region. In Thailand, there's a story about a mermaid who goes up against the god Hanuman but falls for him. In Indonesia, a goddess named Nyal Blorong becomes a mermaid, and there's Nyal Loro Kidu, who's queen of the southern sea.

In the Philippines, what you consider merfolk differs amid cultures. In one, the mermaid is considered to be the queen of the sea who married a mortal and ruled over mankind. In another culture, mermaids were said to have come about from a union of a water god and a water creature. In yet another group, mermaids were known for their beautiful voices (like the Sirens elsewhere)—and vicious personalities. In yet another is a reference to mermaids having two fins. But *sirena* is the general term for mermaids there (and also in the Caribbean! See below) and *siyokoy* for the mermen.

And there are more merfolk myths in the Pacific. There's a well-known Maori story about Pania, which has parallels with merfolk tales around the world. Pania's story, about a woman who swam with the fishes of the reef (thus her usual nickname, "Pania of the Reef") at night off Napier Bay and during the day would swim up a stream to rest. Eventually, she caught the eye of a Maori man and they fell in love. In a variation of what we see all over the world, the man tries to arrange it so she can't go back to the sea—but he fails and she goes home. Now, the sea is protected by Moremore, the son of Pania and the Maori man. Moremore is a taniwha, a sea spirit who most often masquerades as a shark, an octopus, or a stingray.

There's more as we cross the Pacific to the New World, starting north and sailing south:

In 1608, explorer Henry Hudson's crew reported catching a glimpse of a mermaid in the Arctic Ocean (brr!). British Columbia had some sightings between 1870 and 1890. There were five sightings in the Susquehanna River in 1881.

And if you're likely to go to Florida, you can catch professional mermaids (they are; they get paid and everything!) in Weeki Wachee Springs State Park, where you can see performances by female divers. They perform aquatic ballet in an underwater stage with glass walls, ducking every minute or so for breathing devices. Eilis has seen it, and enjoyed the performance. Highly recommended.

Christopher Columbus reported seeing mermaids in the Caribbean (but that was most likely manatees).

The Caribbean has a few merfolk myths, ranging from those of the Neo-Taino's mermaid called Aycaylia, to La Sirene in Haitian voudoun culture.

The wihwin is a nocturnal water spirit in Central America with similarities to the Scottish kelpie and the Australian bunyip. It splits its time between the sea during the winter and the mountains in the summer. It has a taste for human flesh. It has a reputation for being quite unpleasant.

A hop down to Brazil are stories about the iara (or yara), known as "mother of the waters," from the Tupi and Guarani myths. It can also be translated as "lady of the lake," or "water queen." She's known as a water nymph, a siren, or a mermaid who hangs out on the Amazon River. There are stories about her sitting on a rock and sunning herself, and luring men with her song.

And of course, there are pop culture references to merfolk all over the world, in so many variations. There are the movies, and the cartoons, opera, symphonies, and the anime. Merfolk, specifically merrow, have been in games. Merrows can be found in the Harry Potter world, with merrows as one of the subspecies of merfolk.

All of these legends, of course, have inspired other forms of pop culture, too. We go into some of those in Chapter 9, looking at aquatic superheroes.

And this is just a snippet of the folklore out there for merfolk.

Question of the chapter: What would you do if a merperson popped out of the water and said, "Come with me if you want to live!"? I mean, it's a merperson. Wouldn't you need reassurances that there would be some way for you to breathe?

Chapter 9
Aquatic Superheroes

There are some notable water beasties among the comic books:

Marvel Comics's aquatic superhero/antihero, Namor the Sub-Mariner (also known as Namor McKenzie). The first version of Namor was introduced in 1939 as the son of a human sea captain and a princess of the undersea kingdom of Atlantis (yes, one of those many stories inspired by Plato's story), with super-strength and the ability to fly (no, that power's always puzzled me). He's usually depicted as short-tempered and hostile, fighting those who have committed crimes against his kingdom. Come to think of it, Eilis has never actually seen him depicted as being good-natured! (By the time you read this, Namor should have made his appearance in the Marvel Cinematic Universe!)

Marvel Comics's Namor the Sub-Mariner. Detail from a postage stamp.

Then there's Aquaman, the water-based superhero in DC Comics who debuted in 1941, who's been given a number of origins (Eilis found three within seconds of checking three different sources). The character was revived in the early 1960s as a founding member of the Justice League. One of his origins hearkened back to the romantic classics, with his human father, a lighthouse keeper, coming across a beautiful injured woman on his shores during a storm. He nursed her back to health, they fall in love, she reveals that she's actually a mermaid princess from Atlantis, and eventually she goes back to the ocean once she's recovered—but not before she gives birth to a half-human, half-aquatic infant, Arthur Curry, who later discovers he is the king of Atlantis. Since Aquaman's introduction in the 1940s, he's been lauded and laughed at, sometimes derided as useless because he can "only" talk to marine life, sometimes feared because he battles those who would pollute his home (but he never flies). He made his silver screen appearance in 2016 in the form of actor Jason Momoa, looking nothing like the Aquaman Eilis grew up with, but she'll live with that. And the movies (see our Hollywood chapter) are fun. And more to come!

DC Comics's Aquaman. Detail from a postage stamp.

You can speculate why it is that both aquatic superheroes are half-human. Hmm.

Then there are the Sea Devils, which is another DC Comics property. They don't have superpowers, but they do spend most of their time in the sea having adventures. Introduced in 1960, they've been in and out of the DC Universe over the years. (*Doctor Who* has also had "sea devils," amphibious reptiles, show up from time to time in its very long history.)

And here's an aside that's purely personal for Eilis: about Lori Lemaris, a recurring character in DC Comics' Superman stories. A full-blooded mermaid, Lori hails from the city of Tritonis, a city on the submerged continent of Atlantis (the one that Aquaman is the king of), and disguised as a human student in a wheelchair, she met Clark Kent when they were both attending Metropolis University (as seen in *Superman* 129, May 1959). They fell in love and he proposed, but she turned him down and revealed who she really was. Since then, she's popped up from time to time, and she too has had her origins noodled around with.

This is relevant only in that back in the late 1970s, as a college freshman, Eilis sold a story to DC Comics about Lori Lemaris. If you have nothing better to do with your time, you can look up *Action Comics* 475 ("The Weak Link"). At least she thinks that was the title; she wrote some other Superman Family stories, but that was the Lori story (maybe). It was a *long* time ago. That's also when she was inspired to study to become an editor.

Then there's Disney's version of the Little Mermaid, based on Hans Christian Andersen's tale, whom you know as Ariel, the daughter of Trident. Not powerful except as a singer, she's also a greedy little materialistic creature who seems to be a kleptomaniac and falls in love with a landlubber named Eric. Eilis studied folklore (and specifically Andersen), so this version of the character always puzzled her too.

Question of the chapter: Who are your favorite aquatic superheroes?

Have you ever seen a ghost ship?

Chapter 10
Ships of Mystery

The *Flying Dutchman* and *Mary Celeste*! Surely you've heard of these somewhere along the way—they're ghost ships, with strange stories of their own. Before we go to those, though, take a look at some other ghost ship stories:

A Ghost Ship in Wyoming?
Yep, that's right. The Platte River in southeast Wyoming is home to stories about a very bizarre ghost ship. Three times it's been seen and all three times the person witnessed the death of a loved one on the ship—and yes, all three times the loved one died later that very day.

The HMS Queen Mary
Lots of ghosts have been reported to live in the Queen Mary, now docked in Long Beach, California. A man named John Henry worked in the engine room and was killed in a fire. Engine Room 13's door is reportedly often hot to the touch, and there are wisps of smoke reported around it occasionally with nothing to show for it. Many have heard knocking as if someone were trying to get out. Then there are the three female ghosts seen around the pool—one little girl and two women. Psychic Peter James claims that he has communicated with more than a hundred different ghosts on the ships.

And you've been patient, so here's your reward, the story of the *Flying Dutchman*! In case you've sort of heard about the ship (or not at all), it's a legendary ghost ship, doomed never to make port, cursed to sail the sea for all eternity. The oldest story involving the *Dutchman* comes about from the late 1790s, most likely a sea swagger's story. Later stories involving the *Dutchman* has the ship glowing with an eerie light (of course, because why else would we have a ghost ship story)? Catching sight of the ship means doom for those who've seen it, of course.

The origins of this story, most likely, come from a Dutch man-of-war that was lost off the Cape of Good Hope in the 1790s. The first mention described the circumstances of the ship (not given a name in the original source; the "flying Dutchman" reference was a description of the ship, as an apparition that appeared out of nowhere and disappears the same way).

In subsequent references, the legend gained more and more detail, about a common superstitution among sailors that hurricanes are presaged by a ghost ship—the *Flying Dutchman*, as it was now called. The story offered the theory that the crew of the ship was cursed because of a terrible, unspecified crime. The story gained more and more traction, with even Sir Walter Scott adding to the myth, calling it a "pirate ship," having been filled with ill-gotten treasure, and seeing it as a bad omen. Since the story was first told, there have been numerous sightings, including one in the late 19th century by the future George V of Great Britain.

Is the flesh crawling at the back of your neck? It should be. But the way these things go, there's actually a scientific explanation on what the apparition could be: an optical illusion. Certain atmospheric conditions—a mirage—could be the reason why there seems to be a floating ship in the distance. There's also an optical illusion referred to as "looming" that happens when light is bent.

Then there's the *Mary* (or *Marie*) *Celeste*, depending on who's telling this ghost story, another ghost ship—sort of. The *Mary Celeste* incident was almost a century after the myth of the *Flying Dutchman* came about. The ship, a merchant vessel in good condition, was discovered in 1872 in the Atlantic Ocean heading for the Strait of Gibraltar, with no one aboard and one lifeboat missing, even though the weather was fair and the crew veteran sailors. Sir Arthur Conan Doyle, and others, referred to the ship as *"Marie" Celeste* in fictional accounts. While confabulated accounts said that there was food on the table and a pipe still smoking, this was later found out not to be the case, but it was true that most of the cargo was intact (except for some of the alcohol…hmm) and the crew's belongings were still there as well, even though the navigation equipment was reported to be missing. But why the crew and passengers were never seen again has never been confirmed. Underwater earthquakes? Waterspouts? Piracy? Mutiny? A giant kraken? Your guess is as good as anyone else's. But apparently all of the ship's papers were found to be missing except for the captain's logbook, so it's hard to even speculate.

No matter the mystery, the ship eventually met her end when in 1885 her final owner (after the famous incident the ship changed hands *seventeen!* times) wrecked her deliberately off the coast of Haiti in an attempt to commit insurance fraud. The mystery of the *Mary Celeste* has inspired a lot of pop culture, including an episode of *Doctor Who* (back in 1965).

And speaking of pop culture, there's the Blues Image song "Ride Captain Ride," which refers to a "mystery ship," and the lyrics are both mysterious and even sinister:

"Seventy-three men sailed off to history ..."

But what's it mean? According to the cowriters, the band's singer-guitarist Mike Pinera and keyboardist Frank "Skip" Konte, nothing sinister—they needed one more song and they were toodling along, and this is what they came up with. It just sounds portentous! And we don't know about you, but it certainly inspired Eilis to look out at ships and boats whenever she's near the water to search for mystery ships and wonder.

And of course, there's "Wreck of the Edmund Fitzgerald" by Gordon Lightfoot, but that's just about bad weather and a ship falling apart, but one of Eilis's favorites.

Question of the chapter: Did you sing along to either song? Of course you did (if you were of a certain age, at least, or into classic rock & roll). If you were going to add deeper meaning to "Ride Captain Ride," how would you add it?

Chapter 11
Lost Cities and Continents Beneath the Sea

Then of course, we have the mythical cities and continents lost beneath the sea—or perhaps they simply have yet to be found. There's:

Lemuria is a lost continent thought to be located either in the Indian Ocean or Pacific Ocean, but currently, scientists have decided that the plate tectonics of either region they have examined make the existence of Lemuria questionable. Philosopher and occultist Helena Blavatsky claimed in the 1880s that the human population on Lemuria turned to black magic, causing the continent to sink and the gods to create a new race on Atlantis. And speaking of Atlantis…

Atlantis is the name of an island mentioned by Plato within an allegory. At the end of the story, Atlantis "falls out of favor with the gods," so to speak, and sinks into the Atlantic Ocean. From that simple story has risen thousands of works of speculative fiction and nonfiction. It's a name that everyone seems to know. That story itself may have been fiction, but it's still being speculated about what the source of the story was. A volcanic eruption wiping out a civilization? Anyone who remembers that history and the story of Pompeii knows it's very possible. Plato was long gone before Vesuvius blew its top and buried Pompeii, but there are records of eruptions elsewhere even before Plato himself.

Then there's the continent Mu, which was thought to have been in the Pacific Ocean and believed to have sunk into the depths of the sea. Toward the end of the 19th century, scholars Augustus and Alice Le Plongeon proposed the idea that Mu was a lost continent from their study of ancient Mayan writings. There is now some speculation that Mu and Lemuria were actually the same continent. Or not. Further research is required.

There are other stories about countries and cities that sank beneath the sea. There are the stories in Arthurian legend about Lyonesse (also known as "Leonois" or variations), said in some tales to border Cornwall and that can still be heard in the form of bells ringing at certain times of the year nearby. According to Lord Tennyson, Lyonesse is said to be where the final battle between Arthur and Mordred took place. Why, we couldn't find a definitive reason (although in one source it was thought to be a version of Sodom and Gomorrah, and all that wickedness was why it sank).

There are stories about other lost cities and lands in early Celtic tales, including the story of Cité d'Ys (or just Ys), and the Welsh Cantre'r Gwaelod, a legendary submerged kingdom in Cardigan Bay. In some stories, Ys was founded more than two millennia ago off the coast of Breton, but rapidly deteriorated when evil and corruption overcame the city and the Celtic gods sank the place (a variation of the Sodom and Gomorrah story, as in the Lyonesse account).

Then there's Dwarka, which we mentioned in an earlier chapter. It's an existing city in the Indian state of Gujarat, one of four sacred Hindu pilgrimage sites and one of the oldest cities in the Indian subcontinent, but it's also the name of the ancient kingdom-state of Krishna, long thought to be mythical. Recently, however, marine archaeologists have discovered the remains of stone structures that reveal that there would have been a settlement in the earliest historic periods. More underwater research is ongoing.

Question of the chapter: What other lost civilizations and cities can you think of thought to be lost under water?

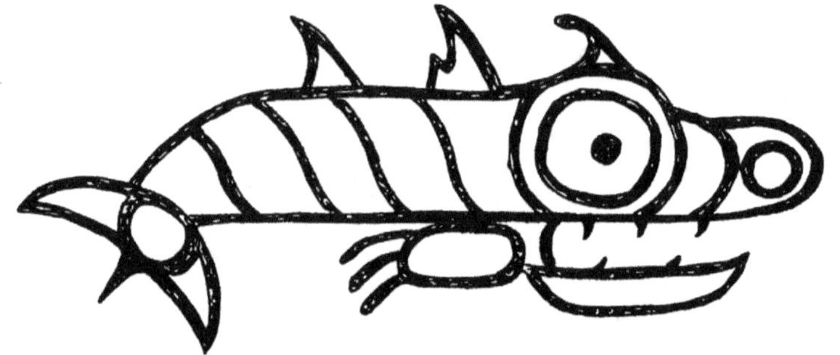

Summary
Where Water Beasties Are Here and There

As we mentioned at the beginning, the waters that make up most of our planet are truly the final frontier. We keep finding things within their depths that we've assumed were long extinct but aren't, we unearth secrets within their depths that continue to surprise, and we know we're nowhere near done. It's only natural that the stories we find and create concerning the waters of the world keep changing and expanding.

Tales of water beasties remind us deep down that water is both life giving and life threatening, in the sense that it can drown you…or keep you alive. When a wayward traveler on the waters comes close to drowning, at some point, you don't know whether they will live or die (in essence, Schrodinger's cat, in the form of a sailor. Possibly Schrodinger's fish), so they are poised between life and death as well. Water not only threatens us and nourishes us, it keeps us in its thrall.

Between the lost continents and cities that sink beneath the waves, and the amazing creatures we have heard about, some extinct, some extant (and some plainly and simply made up), we have no end of things we can imagine and explore when it comes to the seven seas. We are explorers, after all!—Eilis & Jacquie

Bibliography

Andersen, Han Christian [1836]. "The Little Mermaid."

Appiah, Kwame Anthony, and Henry Louis Gates Jr. [1996]. *Dictionary of Global Culture*, Borzoi Books: Alfred A. Knopf, Inc.

Ashe, Geoffrey [1985]. *The Discovery of King Arthur*, Anchor Press/Doubleday.

Atlas Obscura [2022]. "The City of Mermaids—Only in Florida," January 22.

Bacon, Francis. *The New Atlantis*

Bassett, Fletcher S. [1885]. *Legends and Superstitions of the Sea and of Sailors*, Belford, Clarke and Co.

Beatty, Scott; Robert Greenberger; Phil Jimenez; and Dan Wallace. *DC Comics Encyclopedia*

Berger, Knute, and Stephen Hegg [2021]. "Mossback's Northwest: Before the Kraken, what lurked in the Salish Sea?" Crosscut.com.

Berlitz, Charles [1974]. *The Bermuda Triangle*, Wynwood Press.

______ [1989]. *The Dragon's Triangle*, Wynwood Press.

Blavatsky, Helena. *The Secret Doctrine, the Synthesis of Science, Religion and Philosophy*

Bradley, Åsa Maria [2015]. *Viking Warrior Rising*, Sourcebooks.

Briggs, Katharine [1977]. *British Folktales*, Pantheon Books.

Burton, Richard [1850]. *A Thousand and One Nights*.

Campbell, Joseph [1988]. *Myths to Live By*, Bantam Books.

Cavendish, Richard, ed. [1970]. *Man, Myth & Magic: An Illustrated Encyclopedia of the Supernatural*, Marshall Cavendish Corp.

Churchward, James. *The Lost Continent Mu.*

Conway, D.J. [2001]. *Magickal, Mystical Creatures*, Llewellyn Publications.

Cotterell, Arthur [1996]. *Illustrated Encyclopedia of Classical Mythology*, Hermes House.

Curtis, Vesta Sarkhosh [1933]. *Persian Myths*, University of Texas Press.

Davis, F. Hadland [1989]. *Myths & Legends of Japan*, Graham Brash Ltd.

De la Motte Fouqué. *Undine.*

Dieterle, Richard [2005]. *Short Encyclopedia of Hotcâk (Winnebago) Myth, Legend, and Folklore.*

Encyclopedia Mythica

Encyclopaedia Britannica

Erdoes, Richard, and Alfonso Ortiz, eds. [1984]. *American Indian Myths and Legends*, Pantheon Books.

Foster, Michael Dylan [2015]. *The Book of Yokai: Mysterious Creatures of Japanese Folklore,* University of California Press.

Fuller, Edmund [1974]. *Mythology by Thomas Bulfinch*, Dell Publishing.

Galenorn, Yasmine [2014]. "Siobhan and the Siren," *Mist & Shadows*, Nightqueen Enterprises.

Goulart, Ron [2004]. *Comic Book Encyclopedia*, HarperCollins.

Graves, Robert [1960]. *The Greek Myths*, Pelican.

Grossman, Claudia [2020]. *The Mermaid Mahjong Circle: a Fairy Tale for Women*, Gatekeeper Press.

Hamilton, Edith [1969]. *Mythology*, Warner Books.

Homer. *The Iliad and the Odyssey.*

Howe, Sean [2012]. *Marvel Comics: The Untold Story,* HarperCollins.

Internet Movie Database

Ions, Veronica [1992]. *Indian Mythology*, Reed International Books.

Katz, Brian P. [1995]. *Deities and Demons of the Far East*, MetroBooks.

Kidd, Sue Monk [2006]. *The Mermaid Chair*, Penguin.

Knight, Sirona [2005]. *Complete Idiot's Guide to Elves and Fairies*, Penguin Group.

Kuhn, Sarah [2021]. *From Little Tokyo, with Love*, Viking.

Lang, Andrew. *The Brown Fairy Book*

lenntech.com

livescience.com

McCoy, Edain [2006]. *A Witch's Guide to Faery Folk*, Llewellyn Publications.

Mentalfloss.com

Miéville, China [2002]. *The Scar*, Random House.

Murray, Alexander S. [1988]. *Who's Who in Mythology: A Classic Guide to the Ancient World*, Bracken Books.

Mysteriousbritain.co.uk/England/west-sussex/legends

Mythical Beasts [1996]. Anness Publishing, Ltd.

Nivedita, Sister, and Ananda K. Coomararswamy [1994]. *Hindus and Buddhists: Myths and Legends*, Guernsey Press.

Paracelsus. *A Book on Nymphs, Sylphs, Pygnies, and Salamanders.*

Plato. *Timaeus, Critias*

Plini the Elder. *Natural History*

Rowling, J.K. Harry Potter series

Ralston, W.R.S. [1873]. *Russian Folk-Tales*, Elder and Co.

"Ride Captain Ride." Blues Image. Cowriters Mike Pinera and Frank Konte. Atlantic Records.

Roberts, Jeremy [2009]. *Japanese Mythology A to Z*, Chelsea House Publications.

Rogers, Jacquie [2007]. *Faery Special Romances*, Highland Press.

Sacred-texts.com

Schama, Simon [2000]. *A History of Britain: At the Edge of the World? 3000 BC to AD 1603*, Hyperion.

Symbolsage.com.

Smith, Elizabeth M. [1977]. "The Weak Link," *Action* 475, DC Comics.

Storm, Rachel [2002]. *Asian Mythology*, Selectabook Ltd.

Wells, H.G. [1902]. "The Sea Lady."

Wikipedia. Various entries.

Wilde, Oscar [2014]. "The Fisherman and His Soul," HarperPerennial.

Wilkinson, Philip [1998]. *Illustrated Dictionary of Mythology*, DK Publishing.

Worldhistory.org

Yoda, Hiroko, and Matt Alt, trans. [2016]. *Japandemonium Illustrated: The Yokai Encyclopedias of Toriyama Sekien*, Dover Publications.

Illustrations

Silk Road map. Shutterstock
Page 7: Movie poster. Universal Pictures.
Page 16: Cthulu. Creative Commons License
Page 17: Dover Books
Page 19: Sedna. Creative Commons license
Page 23: Rain serpent. Public domain
Page 23: Vision serpent. Public domain
Page 25: Chalchiuhtlicue. Public domain
Page 27: Shutterstock
Page 35: Shutterstock
Page 39: Creative Commons License
Page 40: Shutterstock
Page 41: Creative Commons License
Page 41: Creative Commons License

Author Biographies

ELIZABETH MS FLYNN, who writes as Eilis Flynn, has written fiction in the form of comic book stories, fantasies (romance, urban, and historical), and short stories. She's also a professional editor and has been for more than forty years, working in academia, technology, finance, genre fiction, and comic books. She can be reached at emsflynn.com (if you're looking for an editor) or at eilisflynn.com (if you're looking for a fun read).

JACQUIE ROGERS' first burning desire was to be a baseball announcer, but that didn't work out so she decided to write novels instead. She has written historicals, romances, and award-winning westerns, including the Honey Beaulieu series and the Hearts of Owyhee series.
Website: JacquieRogers.com

Connect with us online
Facebook: www.facebook.com/jacquie.rogers.author
Facebook: www.facebook.com/EilisFlynnAuthor

Jacquie Rogers's website: www.jacquierogers.com
Eilis Flynn's website: www.eilisflynn.com

Have any watery stories you want to share? Have any questions? Ask 'em at mythsalongthesilkroad.blogspot.com!

www.ingramcontent.com/pod-product-compliance
Lightning Source LLC
Chambersburg PA
CBHW051759250726
48659CB00001B/501